Holiday Gifts from the Kitchen

IDEALS PUBLICATIONS INCORPORATED
NASHVILLE, TENNESSEE

CONTENTS

Our sincere thanks to the following companies for their cooperation in supplying recipes and photographs: Alltrista Consumer Products Company, marketers of Ball® home canning products; Dole Food Company; Hershey Foods Corporation; Kellogg Company; Martha White; National Honey Board; The Quaker Oats Company; and Sun-Diamond Growers of California.

Cover Photograph: Cranberry Walnut Conserve, page 29; and Gingered Pears, page 29

A NOTE ON INGREDIENTS AND MEASUREMENTS

In testing the recipes in this cookbook, we have used butter. Generally, margarine can be substituted for butter, but the results may vary from our tested results. The flour used, unless specified otherwise, is general, all-purpose, unbleached flour. The recipes have been tested and were successful under our test conditions.

ISBN 0-8249-5827-6

Photo opposite:
Gingerbread Cookie Kids, page 8; and
Holiday Cookie Surprises, page 9

MARK

CREATIVE COOKIES

STAMPED HOLIDAY COOKIES

Makes about 5 dozen cookies

1 cup butter, softened
1 3-ounce package cream cheese, softened
½ cup sugar
1 tablespoon grated lemon zest
2 cups flour
Carrot Stamps (below)
Sugar

In a large bowl, cream butter and cream cheese with sugar until light and fluffy. Add lemon zest. Gradually stir in flour. Cover and refrigerate 2 hours or until dough is firm. Prepare Carrot Stamps (below). Preheat oven to 375° F. Shape dough into 1-inch balls. Place 2 inches apart on ungreased cookie sheet. Dip ends of Carrot Stamps in sugar and flatten balls to about ¼-inch thickness. Bake 7 to 9 minutes or until edges are firm. Cool on wire racks.

CARROT STAMPS

1 1½-inch diameter carrot

Cut a 1½-inch diameter carrot into 2-inch lengths. Using a small, sharp knife, carve holiday designs (bell, star, etc.) in the ends of carrot pieces. Designs should protrude about ⅛ inch.

RAISIN MOLASSES GEMS

Makes about 3 dozen cookies

2 cups flour
2 teaspoons baking soda
1 teaspoon ground cinnamon
½ teaspoon ground cloves
½ teaspoon ground ginger
¼ teaspoon salt
¾ cup shortening
1 cup sugar
¼ cup molasses
1 egg
1 cup raisins
Sugar

In a small bowl, sift together flour, baking soda, cinnamon, cloves, ginger, and salt. Set aside. In a large bowl, cream shortening with sugar until light and fluffy. Add molasses and egg; blend well. Gradually add flour mixture to molasses mixture, mixing well. Stir in raisins. Cover and refrigerate until firm. Preheat oven to 350° F. Shape dough into 1-inch balls; roll in sugar. Place 2 inches apart on lightly greased cookie sheets. Bake 10 to 12 minutes or until edges are firm. Cool 1 minute; remove to wire racks.

SANTA'S STOCKINGS

Makes about 3 dozen

¾ cup flour
½ teaspoon baking soda
¼ teaspoon salt, optional
½ cup butter, softened
⅔ cup firmly packed brown sugar
¼ cup sugar
1 egg
2 tablespoons milk
1 teaspoon almond extract
2½ cups rolled oats
1 cup dried cherries or cranberries
1 cup coarsely chopped almonds, optional
Decorator's icing
Assorted small candies

Preheat oven to 350° F. In a small bowl, sift together flour, baking soda, and salt. Set aside. In a large bowl, cream butter with sugars until light and fluffy. Add egg, milk, and almond extract; beat well. Stir in flour mixture. Add oats, dried cherries, and almonds; mix well. Divide dough into 4 equal portions. With moistened hands, pat dough onto lightly greased cookie sheets into ¼-inch thick holiday shapes such as stockings, Christmas trees, or candy canes. Bake 12 to14 minutes or until edges are light golden brown. Cool 2 minutes on cookie sheet; carefully remove to wire racks. Cool completely. Decorate as desired with tubed decorator's icing and small, colored candies. Store in tightly covered container.

Blondies

Makes about 20 bars

5 tablespoons butter, softened
1 cup firmly packed brown sugar
1 teaspoon vanilla
1 egg
1 cup flour
¾ teaspoon baking powder
¼ teaspoon salt
1 cup chopped walnuts, divided

Preheat oven to 350° F. In a large bowl, cream butter with brown sugar until light and fluffy. Add vanilla and egg, mixing well. Set aside. In a small bowl, sift together flour, baking powder, and salt. Stir into butter mixture, mixing well. Fold in ¾ cup of the walnuts. Spread dough evenly in a greased 8-inch square pan. Sprinkle with remaining ¼ cup walnuts. Bake 30 minutes or until edges are lightly browned. Cool and cut into bars.

Thumbprint Cookies

Makes about 2 dozen cookies

½ cup butter, softened
½ cup sugar
1 egg, separated
½ teaspoon vanilla
1 cup flour
¼ teaspoon salt
1 cup finely chopped walnuts
Jam or candied cherries

Preheat oven to 350° F. In a large bowl, cream butter with sugar until light and fluffy. Stir in egg yolk and vanilla, mixing well. Add flour and salt, mixing well. Shape dough into 1-inch balls. Slightly beat egg white. Dip balls in egg white and roll in walnuts. Place balls 1 inch apart on ungreased cookie sheet. Press thumb gently in the center of each cookie. Bake 10 to 12 minutes or until firm. Cool on wire racks. Fill thumbprints with jam or candied cherries.

Note: For Chocolate Thumbprints, melt one 1-ounce square unsweetened chocolate and stir into butter mixture. Fill thumbprints with candied cherries.

Acorn Cookies

Makes about 4½ dozen cookies

3½ cups flour
1 teaspoon baking powder
¼ teaspoon salt
1 cup butter, softened
1 cup sugar
½ cup milk
1 teaspoon vanilla
1 teaspoon almond extract
1 egg
1 12-ounce package semisweet chocolate chips
2 cups finely chopped nuts

In a small bowl, sift together flour, baking powder, and salt. Set aside. In a large bowl, cream butter with sugar until light and fluffy. Stir in milk, vanilla, almond extract, and egg. Gradually add flour mixture to butter mixture, mixing well after each addition. Cover and refrigerate at least 4 hours. Preheat oven to 375° F. Shape dough into 2-inch ovals. Pinch 1 end of oval into a point to resemble an acorn. Place 1 inch apart on ungreased cookie sheet. Bake 9 to 12 minutes or until edges are firm. Immediately remove from cookie sheet. Cool completely on wire rack. In a saucepan, heat chocolate chips, stirring constantly, until melted. Dip about ⅓ of wide, rounded end of each cookie into chocolate; dip into nuts. Place cookies on waxed paper until chocolate is set.

Wrapping Hint

Make a show-off gift box for Christmas cookies from a greeting card box with a transparent plastic lid. Cover the bottom of the box with Christmas wrapping paper. Tie with bright ribbon.

Packing Hint

Soft bar and drop cookies usually travel well. Rolled or pressed cookies break easily—they may become crumbs before the recipient gets them. Pack cookies of the same variety together. Otherwise the flavors will mingle and the distinctive taste of each kind will be lost.

Chocolate Banana Biscotti

Makes about 4 dozen cookies

- **4 cups flour**
- **2 teaspoons baking powder**
- **½ teaspoon salt**
- **¼ cup butter, softened**
- **1½ cups sugar**
- **2 eggs**
- **2 medium, ripe bananas, mashed**
- **1 teaspoon vanilla**
- **1 cup whole toasted almonds**
- **2 cups white or milk chocolate chips**

Preheat oven to 325° F. In a small bowl, sift together flour, baking powder, and salt; set aside. In a large bowl, cream butter with sugar until light and fluffy. Add eggs, banana, and vanilla, beating until well blended. Gradually add flour mixture and almonds, mixing well. Turn out on a floured board and divide dough in half. Form each half into 12- x 3-inch rolls. Place 3 inches apart on lightly greased cookie sheet. Bake 25 to 30 minutes or until firm and lightly browned. Cool on wire racks for 15 minutes. Slice each log diagonally into ½-inch thick slices. Place slices on cookie sheet and bake 10 more minutes. Turn slices over; bake 10 to 15 minutes more until lightly browned on top and bottom. Remove to wire rack and cool completely. Biscotti will become crispier as they cool. Melt chocolate. Spread or drizzle melted chocolate on top of each biscotti. Chill 10 minutes or until chocolate is firm. Store in airtight containers.

Chocolate Raisin Crinkles

Makes 3½ dozen cookies

- **½ cup butter, softened**
- **1⅔ cups sugar**
- **1 tablespoon vanilla**
- **2 ounces unsweetened chocolate squares, melted**
- **2 cups flour**
- **2 teaspoons baking powder**
- **¼ teaspoon salt**
- **⅓ cup milk**
- **1 cup raisins**
- **Powdered sugar**

In a large bowl, cream butter with sugar until light and fluffy. Add vanilla. Blend in melted chocolate. Set aside. In a small bowl, sift together flour, baking powder, and salt; add to chocolate mixture alternately with milk, stirring after each addition. Stir in raisins. Cover and refrigerate until firm. Preheat oven to 350° F. Shape dough into 1-inch balls; roll in powdered sugar. Place 2 inches apart on greased cookie sheets. Bake 12 to 15 minutes.

Snickerdoodles

Makes about 3½ dozen cookies

- **2¾ cups flour**
- **1½ teaspoons cream of tartar**
- **1 teaspoon baking soda**
- **¼ teaspoon salt**
- **1 cup butter, softened**
- **1½ cups sugar**
- **2 eggs**
- **1½ cups raisins**
- **2 tablespoons sugar mixed with 2 teaspoons cinnamon**

Preheat oven to 375° F. In a small bowl, sift together flour, cream of tartar, baking soda, and salt. Set aside. In a large mixing bowl, cream butter with sugar until light and fluffy. Add eggs, blending well. Gradually add flour mixture, mixing well. Stir in raisins. Shape dough into 1-inch balls, then roll in sugar and cinnamon mixture. Place balls 2 inches apart on greased cookie sheets. Bake 10 to 12 minutes or until edges are firm. Cool on wire racks.

Gift Hint

Any rolled cookie can be made into a Christmas tree ornament. Cut a piece of string or thread for each cookie. Place the string on the top of the cut cookie on the sheet and press into the dough. Bake as usual.

Photo opposite:
Kris Kringle Fudge Cookies , page 8

Christmas is
A time to care

Gingerbread Cookie Kids

Makes about 2 dozen cookies

3⅓ cups flour
½ teaspoon baking soda
1 teaspoon ground cinnamon
1 teaspoon ground ginger
½ teaspoon ground nutmeg
½ teaspoon salt, optional
1½ cups rolled oats
1 cup butter, softened
¾ cup firmly packed brown sugar
½ cup molasses
1 egg
Prepared frosting or decorator's icing
Assorted small candies

In a small bowl, sift together flour, baking soda, spices, and salt; stir in oats. Set aside. In a large mixing bowl, cream butter with sugar until light and fluffy. Add molasses and egg, beating well. Add flour mixture, a little at a time, mixing well. Divide dough into 2 portions for easier handling. Cover with plastic wrap; chill 2 hours. Preheat oven to 350° F. On a lightly floured board, roll dough ¼ inch thick. Cut with a 5-inch gingerbread cookie cutter. Place 2 inches apart on ungreased cookie sheet. Bake 8 to 10 minutes or until lightly browned. Cool on wire racks. Decorate cooled cookies with frosting, using candies as eyes, mouth, and nose. Store in tightly covered container.

Kris Kringle Fudge Cookies

Makes about 2½ dozen cookies

1 cup flour, divided
1 cup sugar
1 teaspoon baking soda
¼ teaspoon salt
⅓ cup cocoa
¼ cup butter, melted
2 eggs
1 teaspoon vanilla
¼ cup chopped pecans
Powdered sugar

In a small bowl, sift together ½ cup of the flour and the sugar, baking soda, and salt. Set aside. In a large bowl, stir cocoa into melted butter. Cool slightly. Add eggs and vanilla and stir well. Add flour mixture; beat until well blended. Stir in remaining ½ cup flour and pecans; mix well. Cover and refrigerate about 3 hours or until firm. Preheat oven to 300° F. Shape dough into 1-inch balls; roll in powdered sugar. Place 3-inches apart on greased cookie sheet. Bake 10 to 12 minutes until tops have crackled appearance and edges are firm.

Pfeffernuesse

Makes about 4½ dozen cookies

2 cups flour
2 teaspoons baking powder
1 teaspoon ground cinnamon
½ teaspoon ground nutmeg
¼ teaspoon ground cloves
2 teaspoons butter, softened
1 cup sugar
2 eggs
1 teaspoon water
¾ cup currants
Icing (below) or powdered sugar
Dash cinnamon

Preheat oven to 350° F. In a small bowl, sift together flour, baking powder, cinnamon, nutmeg, and cloves. Set aside. In a large bowl, cream butter with sugar until light and fluffy. Add eggs and water, blending well. Stir flour mixture into butter mixture, mixing well. Fold in currants. Shape dough into 1-inch balls. Place 2 inches apart on greased cookie sheets. Bake 10 minutes or until edges are golden. Cool on wire racks. Dip cooled cookies in Icing (below) to lightly coat. Place on waxed paper and let stand until icing is firm. Or dust cookies with powdered sugar. Sprinkle cinnamon over all. Store in an airtight container up to 1 month.

Icing

2 egg whites
2 teaspoons light corn syrup
2 cups powdered sugar

In a small bowl, combine all ingredients; blend well.

Gingersnaps

Makes about 4 dozen cookies

- **2¼ cups flour**
- **2 teaspoons baking soda**
- **1 teaspoon ground cinnamon**
- **1 teaspoon ground ginger**
- **½ teaspoon ground cloves**
- **¼ teaspoon salt**
- **1 cup firmly packed brown sugar**
- **¾ cup shortening**
- **¼ cup molasses**
- **1 egg**
- **Sugar**

In a small bowl, sift together flour, baking soda, cinnamon, ginger, cloves, and salt. Set aside. In a large bowl, cream brown sugar with shortening until light and fluffy. Add molasses and egg, mixing well. Stir in flour mixture. Cover and refrigerate at least 1 hour. Preheat oven to 375° F. Shape teaspoonfuls of dough into balls. Dip top of each ball in granulated sugar. Place balls, sugared sides up, 3 inches apart on greased cookie sheet. Bake 9 to 12 minutes or until edges are firm. Cool on wire racks.

Mocha Macaroons

Makes about 3½ dozen cookies

- **2 tablespoons baking cocoa**
- **3 egg whites**
- **1 teaspoon dry instant coffee powder**
- **¼ teaspoon cream of tartar**
- **⅛ teaspoon salt**
- **½ cup sugar**
- **2 cups flaked coconut**

Preheat oven to 300° F. In a small bowl, stir cocoa until smooth and powdery; set aside. In a medium bowl, combine egg whites, coffee, cream of tartar, and salt. Beat with electric mixer on high speed until foamy. With mixer on high, add sugar, 1 tablespoon at a time. Continue beating until stiff peaks form. Fold cocoa and coconut into meringue. Drop rounded teaspoonfuls 1 inch apart onto a lightly greased cookie sheet. Bake 20 to 25 minutes or until edges are firm. Cool 10 minutes; remove to wire racks. Sift additional cocoa over top of macaroons if desired.

Holiday Sugar Cookies

Makes about 7 dozen cookies

- **3 cups flour**
- **1 teaspoon salt**
- **½ teaspoon baking soda**
- **1 cup butter, softened**
- **1 cup sugar**
- **1½ teaspoons vanilla**
- **2 eggs**

In a small bowl, sift together flour, salt, and baking soda. Set aside. In a large bowl, cream butter with sugar until light and fluffy; add vanilla and eggs, mixing well. Add flour mixture and stir well. Divide dough into 3 equal parts. Shape each part into a roll about 1½ inches in diameter. Wrap each roll with plastic wrap and refrigerate at least 4 hours. Preheat oven to 400° F. Cut rolls into ⅛-inch slices. Place 1 inch apart on ungreased cookie sheets. Bake 8 to 10 minutes or until edges are golden. Remove to wire racks to cool.

Holiday Cookie Surprises

Makes about 4 dozen cookies

- **1 cup butter, softened**
- **1½ cups powdered sugar, divided**
- **1 egg**
- **1 teaspoon vanilla**
- **2 cups flour**
- **1¼ cups uncooked oats**
- **¼ teaspoon salt (optional)**
- **48 assorted bite-sized candies (candy-coated chocolate bits, jelly beans, gum drops)**
- **Colored sugar, nonpareils, or sprinkles**

Preheat oven to 325° F. In a large bowl, cream butter with sugar until light and fluffy. Add egg and vanilla, beating well. Set aside. In a small bowl, combine flour, oats, and salt. Add flour mixture to butter mixture, mixing well. Shape dough into 1-inch balls. Press a bite-sized candy piece into the center of each ball and shape dough around candy so it is completely hidden. Roll balls in colored sugar, nonpareils, or sprinkles until evenly coated. Bake on ungreased cookie sheet 14 to 17 minutes or until edges are golden. Cool on wire racks 5 minutes. Sprinkle cookies with remaining powdered sugar or shake with sugar in a bag. Store in tightly covered containers.

Lemon Refrigerator Cookies

Makes about 5 dozen cookies

- 1½ cups flour
- ½ teaspoon baking soda
- ¾ teaspoon salt
- ½ cup butter
- 1 cup sugar
- 1 egg
- 1 teaspoon lemon juice
- 2 teaspoons grated lemon zest

Preheat oven to 400° F. In a small bowl, sift together flour, baking soda, and salt. Set aside. Cream butter with sugar until light and fluffy. Stir in egg, lemon juice, and zest. Gradually add dry ingredients, mixing well. Divide dough in half; shape each half into a long smooth roll, about 2 inches in diameter. Wrap rolls in plastic wrap and chill until firm enough to slice easily. Slice cookies ⅛-inch thick. Place on ungreased, foil-covered cookie sheets. Bake for 6 to 8 minutes until lightly browned.

Butterscotch Crisps

Makes about 3½ dozen cookies

- 1 cup flour
- 1 teaspoon baking soda
- ¼ teaspoon salt
- 1 12-ounce package butterscotch-flavored chips, divided
- ¾ cup butter
- ¾ cup sugar
- 1 egg
- 2 cups rolled oats
- 1 cup chopped walnuts

Preheat oven to 350° F. In a small bowl, sift together flour, baking soda, and salt. Set aside. In a small saucepan, combine 1 cup of the butterscotch chips with butter. Stir over low heat until melted and smooth. Remove from heat and cool 5 minutes. Transfer mixture to a large bowl. Add sugar and egg; beat until creamy. Gradually stir in oats and flour mixture; mix well. Fold in remaining 1 cup butterscotch chips and walnuts. Drop by rounded tablespoonfuls onto ungreased cookie sheets. Bake 10 to 12 minutes or until edges are golden. Cool on wire racks.

Raisin Oaties

Makes about 3 dozen cookies

- 2 cups flour
- 1 teaspoon baking soda
- ¼ teaspoon salt
- 1 cup butter, softened
- ¾ cup sugar
- ¾ cup firmly packed brown sugar
- 2 eggs
- 1½ teaspoons vanilla
- 2 cups rolled oats
- 1 cup chopped walnuts
- 1 cup raisins

Preheat oven to 350° F. In a small bowl, sift together flour, baking soda, and salt. Set aside. In a large mixing bowl, cream butter with sugars until light and fluffy. Stir in eggs and vanilla, mixing well. Gradually add flour mixture to butter mixture, mixing well. Stir in oats, walnuts, and raisins. Drop dough by tablespoonfuls onto greased cookie sheets. Bake 10 to 12 minutes or until lightly browned. Cool on wire racks.

Best Chocolate Chip Cookies

Makes about 5 dozen cookies

- 3 cups flour
- 1 teaspoon baking soda
- ½ teaspoon salt
- 1 cup butter, softened
- 1⅓ cups sugar
- ⅔ cup firmly packed brown sugar
- 2 eggs
- 1½ teaspoons vanilla
- 1 12-ounce package semisweet chocolate chips
- 2 cups chopped walnuts

Preheat oven to 350° F. In a small bowl, sift together flour, baking soda, and salt. Set aside. In a large mixing bowl, cream butter with sugars until light and fluffy. Add eggs and vanilla; mix well. Fold in chocolate chips and walnuts. Drop dough by tablespoonfuls onto ungreased cookie sheets. Bake 10 minutes or until edges are firm. Cool on wire racks. Store in airtight containers.

Photo opposite:
Chocolate Banana Biscotti, page 6

Dole

ERFECT PIES

Mocha-Walnut Fudge Pie

Makes 8 servings

- ¼ cup butter, softened
- ¾ cup firmly packed brown sugar
- 3 eggs
- 1 12-ounce package semisweet chocolate chips, melted
- 2 teaspoons instant coffee powder
- 1 teaspoon vanilla
- ¼ cup flour
- 1 cup chopped walnuts
- ½ cup walnut halves
- 1 9-inch unbaked pie shell
- Whipped cream, optional

Preheat oven to 375° F. In a large bowl, cream butter with brown sugar until light and fluffy. Add eggs, one at a time, beating well after each addition. Add chocolate, instant coffee, and vanilla. Mix well. Stir in flour and 1 cup chopped walnuts. Pour into pie shell. Arrange walnut halves attractively on top. Bake for 25 minutes. Cool on wire rack. Serve chilled and topped with whipped cream, if desired. Store in refrigerator.

Basic Pie Pastry

Makes one 9-inch double-crust pie. For single-crust pie, use half the recipe.

- 1¼ cups flour
- ½ teaspoon salt
- ½ cup vegetable shortening
- 3 to 4 tablespoons cold water

In a medium bowl, combine flour and salt. Using a pastry blender, cut in half of the shortening until mixture resembles cornmeal. Cut in remaining shortening until mixture resembles small peas. Add water, a tablespoon at a time, mixing with a fork, until dough forms a ball. On a lightly floured board, roll out half the dough into a circle about 2 inches larger than the pie plate. Ease into plate. Roll other half out, cut vents in top, fold in quarters, and gently unfold over top of pie. Fill according to recipe.

French Apple Raisin Pie

Makes 8 servings

- 4 cups (4 to 6 medium) peeled, chopped tart apples
- 1 tablespoon lemon juice
- 1½ cups raisins
- 1 cup water
- ½ cup sugar
- 1 tablespoon plus ¾ cup flour, divided
- ½ teaspoon ground cinnamon
- ¼ teaspoon salt
- 1 9-inch unbaked pie shell
- ½ cup firmly packed brown sugar
- ⅓ cup butter

Preheat oven to 425° F. If apples lack tartness, sprinkle with lemon juice. In a small saucepan, combine raisins and water. Bring to a boil over high heat. Boil 5 to 7 minutes or until liquid is almost absorbed. In a small bowl, combine sugar, 1 tablespoon flour, cinnamon, and salt, mixing well. Stir into raisin mixture. Pour raisin mixture over apples, tossing to mix. Pour into pie shell. In a small bowl, combine remaining ¾ cup flour and brown sugar. Using a pastry blender, cut in butter until mixture is crumbly. Sprinkle crumbs evenly over raisin-apple mixture. Bake 10 minutes. Reduce temperature to 350° F. Bake an additional 45 to 55 minutes or until golden brown. Serve warm or cold.

Traditional Chess Pie

Makes 8 servings

- ½ cup butter, softened
- 1 cup sugar
- ¼ cup sweetened condensed milk
- 2 eggs, beaten
- 1 teaspoon vanilla
- 1 cup chopped walnuts
- 1 cup raisins
- 1 9-inch unbaked pie shell

Preheat oven to 325° F. In a large bowl, cream butter with sugar until light and fluffy. Stir in sweetened condensed milk, eggs, and vanilla, mixing well. Fold in walnuts and raisins. Pour into pie shell. Bake 60 minutes. Cool before serving.

Noreen's Favorite Walnut Pie

Makes 8 servings

- **3 eggs, slightly beaten**
- **1 cup sugar**
- **2 tablespoons flour**
- **1 cup dark corn syrup**
- **2 tablespoons butter, melted**
- **1 teaspoon vanilla**
- **1 9-inch unbaked pie shell**
- **1½ cups coarsely chopped walnuts**

Preheat oven to 400° F. In a large bowl, combine eggs, sugar, flour, corn syrup, butter, and vanilla. Blend well. Pour into unbaked pie shell. Arrange walnuts on top of mixture. Bake 15 minutes. Reduce oven temperature to 350° F. Bake an additional 35 to 45 minutes or until center is set. Cool completely.

Lemon Delight Pie

Makes 8 servings

- **1 tablespoon cornstarch**
- **3 cups plus 2 tablespoons water, divided**
- **1 cup raisins**
- **½ cup plus 3 tablespoons sugar, divided**
- **1 3-ounce package lemon pudding and pie filling mix**
- **2 egg yolks**
- **1 cup sour cream**
- **1 9-inch baked pie shell**

In a small bowl, combine cornstarch and 2 tablespoons water, stirring until smooth and cornstarch is dissolved. Set aside. In a small saucepan, combine raisins, 3 tablespoons sugar, and 1 cup water. Over medium heat, simmer 15 minutes, stirring occasionally. Slowly pour in cornstarch mixture; stirring constantly, cook until thickened. Remove from heat and set aside. In a large saucepan, combine pie filling mix and remaining ½ cup sugar. Stir in remaining 2 cups water and egg yolks; blend well. Place over medium heat, stirring constantly, until mixture comes to a full boil. Remove from heat and stir in raisin mixture. Cool to lukewarm. Fold in sour cream; pour into pie shell. Cover with plastic wrap or foil and refrigerate several hours.

Pink Peppermint Pie

Makes 8 servings

- **24 large marshmallows**
- **½ cup milk**
- **1 teaspoon vanilla**
- **⅛ teaspoon salt**
- **6 drops peppermint extract**
- **6 drops red food color**
- **1 cup whipping cream**
- **1 9-inch Graham Cracker Pie Shell (below)**
- **2 tablespoons crushed, hard peppermint candy**

In a 3-quart saucepan, combine marshmallows and milk. Heat over low heat, stirring constantly, just until marshmallows are melted. Remove from heat. Stir in vanilla, salt, peppermint extract, and food color. Refrigerate uncovered, stirring occasionally, until mixture mounds slightly when dropped from a spoon. In a chilled small bowl, beat whipping cream until stiff. Fold whipped cream into marshmallow mixture. Spread in baked Graham Cracker Pie Shell (below). Freeze uncovered about 3 hours or until completely frozen. Wrap, label, and return to freezer. Store up to 2 months. A half hour before serving, remove pie from freezer. Thaw in wrapper at room temperature. Just before serving, sprinkle with crushed candy.

Graham Cracker Pie Shell

Makes single crust for 9-inch pie

- **1½ cups graham cracker crumbs (about 20 squares)**
- **⅓ cup butter, melted**
- **3 tablespoons sugar**

Preheat oven to 350° F. In a large bowl, combine all ingredients and mix well. Press mixture firmly into bottom and sides of a 9-inch pie plate. Bake 10 minutes.

Packing Hint

When mailing food packages, type or print the label and enclose an extra address label inside the package. Be sure to use adequate postage and mark the package "Fragile." If you wish, decorate the outside of the box with bright holiday stickers.

Frozen Chocolate-Almond Pie

Makes 8 servings

- 1 **quart chocolate ice cream, softened**
- 1 **cup whipping cream, whipped**
- 1 **teaspoon vanilla**
- 1 **teaspoon almond extract**
- 1 **9-inch Toasted Almond Crust, chilled (below)**
- ¼ **cup toasted slivered almonds, for garnish**

In a large bowl, combine ice cream, whipped cream, vanilla, and almond extract; quickly mix until blended. Pour into pie shell, cover with foil, and freeze 1½ to 3 hours. Sprinkle with almonds before serving.

Note: For Frozen Pistachio-Almond Pie, follow directions above, but use 1 quart pistachio or macaroon ice cream, 1 cup whipping cream, and 1 teaspoon almond extract. Garnish with toasted slivered almonds and 12 maraschino cherry halves.

Toasted Almond Crust

Makes single crust for 9-inch pie

- ½ **cup butter**
- ½ **cup chopped almonds**
- ½ **cup sugar**
- 1 **cup flour**
- ¼ **teaspoon ground cinnamon**

Melt butter in large skillet; stir in almonds and sauté until golden. Remove from heat; stir in sugar, flour, and cinnamon until mixture is golden and crumbly. Press into a 9-inch pie plate. Chill 2 hours before filling.

Wrapping Hint

Dried flowers look especially nice as decorations for wrapped gifts from your kitchen. In midsummer, look for Queen Anne's lace to dry. It makes a delicate and attractive addition to a package. Pick the flowers when fresh and hang right-side up but with the blossoms protected by chicken wire. Cover the top of the flower with paper to prevent it from curling, and let flowers dry at least a week or two. Store in an airtight container until needed to decorate a gift.

Sweet Potato Pie

Makes 8 servings

- ¼ **cup butter, softened**
- ⅔ **cup firmly packed dark brown sugar**
- 4 **eggs**
- ¾ **cup dark corn syrup**
- 1 **teaspoon vanilla**
- 1 **cup mashed, cooked sweet potatoes**
- 1 **cup chopped pecans**
- 1 **unbaked pie shell**
- **Pecan halves for garnish**
- **Whipped cream, optional**

Preheat oven to 400° F. In a large bowl, cream butter with brown sugar until light and fluffy. Add eggs, one at a time, beating well after each addition. Blend in corn syrup, vanilla, sweet potatoes, and chopped pecans. Pour into pie shell. Bake 10 minutes. Reduce oven temperature to 350° F. Bake an additional 30 minutes or until filling is set and crust is golden. Cool on wire rack. Garnish with pecans. Serve with whipped cream, if desired.

Apple-Nut Cobbler Pie

Makes 8 servings

- **Pastry for single-crust 9-inch pie**
- 1½ **cups sugar, divided**
- ½ **teaspoon ground cinnamon**
- ¼ **teaspoon ground nutmeg**
- ¾ **cup chopped walnuts, divided**
- 4 **cups pared, thinly sliced tart apples**
- 1 **cup flour**
- 1 **teaspoon baking powder**
- ¼ **teaspoon salt**
- 1 **egg, beaten**
- ½ **cup milk**
- ⅓ **cup butter, melted**

Preheat oven to 450° F. Butter a 2-quart round casserole; roll pastry and line bottom of casserole. Prick pastry with tines of fork; bake 5 minutes. Reduce oven temperature to 325° F. Combine ½ cup of the sugar and the cinnamon, nutmeg, and half the walnuts. Arrange apples on pastry; sprinkle with sugar mixture. In a small bowl, sift together flour, remaining 1 cup sugar, baking powder, and salt. Add egg, milk, and melted butter; stir until smooth. Pour over apples. Sprinkle with remaining walnuts. Bake 50 to 55 minutes.

Photo opposite: Cherry-Almond Topped Fudge, page 17; Decadent Holiday Chocolate Torte, page 25

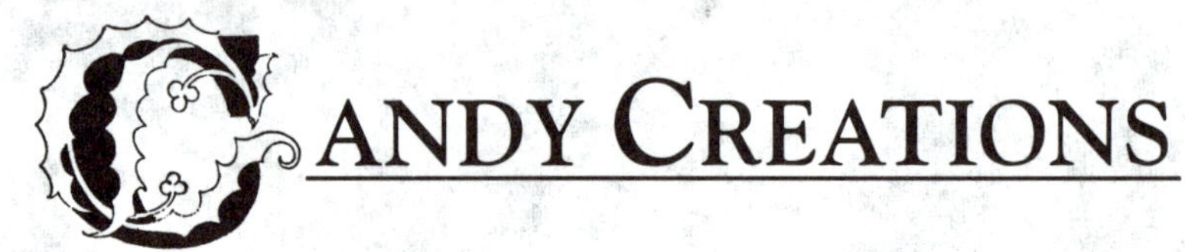

Candy Creations

Toffee Bars

Makes about 2 dozen bars

1 cup butter, softened
1 cup firmly packed brown sugar
1 egg yolk
1 teaspoon vanilla
2 cups flour
1 cup chopped walnuts, divided
½ cup semisweet chocolate chips

Preheat oven to 350° F. In a large bowl, cream butter with brown sugar until light and fluffy. Stir in egg yolk and vanilla. Add flour and ½ cup of the walnuts, stirring to mix well. Spread in a greased 13- x 9-inch pan. Bake 25 minutes or until lightly browned. Immediately sprinkle with chocolate chips and spread as they melt. Sprinkle chocolate with remaining ½ cup walnuts. Cool completely and cut into bars.

Nutty Crispy Crunch Bars

Makes 24 bars

¼ cup butter
½ cup peanut butter
1 10-ounce package large marshmallows
5 cups toasted rice cereal
1½ cups raisins

In a large saucepan, melt butter. Stir in peanut butter. Add marshmallows and cook over low heat, stirring constantly, until melted. Remove from heat and stir in cereal and raisins, mixing well. Press mixture into a buttered 13- x 9-inch pan. Cool completely and cut into bars.

Chocolate-covered Candy Canes

Makes 16 candy canes

½ cup semisweet chocolate chips
2 teaspoons shortening
16 6-inch peppermint candy canes or sticks
Crushed hard peppermint candy or semisweet mini chips

Line a 15½- x 10½- x 1-inch jelly roll pan with waxed paper. In a 1-quart saucepan, combine chocolate chips and shortening. Heat over low heat until melted. Tip saucepan, allowing chocolate to run up the side. Dip one candy cane at a time into chocolate, coating about ¾ of each stick with chocolate. Place in lined pan. Let stand about 2 minutes or until chocolate is partially dry. Roll chocolate-dipped ends in crushed peppermint candy. Let stand about 10 minutes or until chocolate is dry. Store loosely covered at room temperature up to 2 weeks.

Fantasy Fudge

Makes 2½ pounds fudge

1⅓ cups sugar
1 5-ounce can evaporated milk
¼ cup butter
1 7-ounce jar marshmallow creme
1 12-ounce package semisweet chocolate chips
1 teaspoon vanilla
1½ cups coarsely chopped walnuts, optional

In a 2-quart saucepan, combine sugar, milk, butter, and marshmallow creme. Bring to a full boil over medium heat, stirring constantly. Boil exactly 5 minutes over moderate heat, stirring constantly. Remove from heat; add chocolate chips and vanilla. Stir until chocolate is melted. Stir in walnuts; pour into buttered 8-inch square pan. Let stand until firm; cut into squares.

Rocky Road

Makes 1½ pounds candy

1 pound milk chocolate, broken or chopped
2 cups miniature marshmallows
1½ cups coarsely chopped walnuts

Place chocolate in a 2-quart glass measuring bowl with handle. Microwave at high (100%) for 2 to 2½ minutes. Stir until melted. Fold in marshmallows and walnuts, stirring until well mixed. Pour into buttered 8-inch square pan. Refrigerate until set. Cut into squares.

Creamy Butter Fudge

Makes approximately 50 pieces

- 3 cups sugar
- ½ cup cocoa
- ⅛ teaspoon salt
- 1 tablespoon unflavored gelatin
- 1 cup whipping cream
- ½ cup milk
- ¼ cup light corn syrup
- ½ cup butter
- ½ cup margarine
- 1½ teaspoons vanilla
- 1½ cups chopped walnuts or pecans

In a heavy 4-quart saucepan, combine all ingredients except vanilla and nuts. Mix well and bring to a rolling boil. Continue to cook, stirring constantly, to 238° F on a candy thermometer. Gradually lower heat and stir gently. Remove from heat; pour into a bowl. Cool 20 minutes; add vanilla and beat with mixer on low speed until creamy. Stir in nuts. Spread in a 9-inch square pan. Cool and cut into squares.

Cherry-Almond Topped Fudge

Makes about 4 dozen squares

- 1 8-ounce can almond paste
- 1 14-ounce can sweetened condensed milk, divided
- Few drops red food color
- 1¾ cups semisweet chocolate chips, or one 10-ounce package semisweet chocolate chunks
- Red candied cherries, halved
- Sliced almonds

Line an 8-inch square pan with foil. In a small bowl, combine almond paste and ¼ cup of the sweetened condensed milk; mix well. Add food color; beat until well blended. Refrigerate until stiff, about 1 hour. Spread in the bottom of prepared pan. In a small saucepan, combine chocolate and remaining condensed milk. Place over low heat just until chocolate is melted and mixture is smooth when stirred. Spread over top of almond paste layer. Cover and refrigerate until firm. Invert pan onto cutting board; peel off foil. Cut in squares; garnish with candied cherry halves and sliced almonds. Store in refrigerator.

Gift Idea

Place a batch of chocolate-covered candy canes alongside a festive tree ornament in a holiday tin to make the perfect hostess gift for your next tree-trimming party.

Honey Popcorn Clusters

Makes 7 cups

- 6 cups air-popped popcorn
- ⅔ cup seedless or golden raisins
- ½ cup chopped dates
- ⅓ cup slivered almonds, optional
- ⅓ cup packed brown sugar
- ¼ cup honey
- 2 tablespoons butter
- ¼ teaspoon baking soda

Preheat oven to 300° F. Line bottom and sides of a 13- x 9-inch baking pan with aluminum foil. Spray foil with vegetable cooking spray. In a large bowl, combine popcorn, raisins, dates, and almonds. Spread in foil-lined pan. In a small saucepan, combine brown sugar, honey, and butter. Bring to a boil over medium heat, stirring constantly; reduce heat to low. Cook 5 minutes; do not stir. Remove from heat. Stir in baking soda. Drizzle over popcorn mixture, stirring quickly to coat mixture evenly. Bake for 12 to 15 minutes or until lightly browned, stirring once halfway through baking. Lift foil from pan; place on cooling rack. Cool completely. Break into clusters. Store in airtight container for up to 1 week.

Packing Hint

Old-fashioned apothecary jars make excellent gift containers for homemade candies. They are available in different colors, but use clear jars for your brightest candies.

Holiday Wreaths

Makes 8 wreaths

- ½ cup butter
- 40 large marshmallows
- 1½ teaspoons green food color
- 6 cups cornflake cereal
- Red cinnamon candy
- Red lace licorice
- Prepared frosting

In a large glass bowl, combine butter and marshmallows. Place bowl in microwave oven and cook at high power (100%) for 2 minutes. Remove from microwave and stir mixture with spatula. Return to microwave and cook for an additional 2 minutes on high power. Stir mixture until smooth. Add food color and stir to blend completely. Add cereal to warm marshmallow mixture. Using buttered spatula, stir until cereal is well coated; cool until easy to handle. Using a lightly greased ½ cup measure, divide cereal mixture into 8 portions. With buttered hands, form each measure into a wreath. Decorate with cinnamon candy. Cut licorice into 12-inch pieces. Tie licorice into bows. Attach bows to wreaths with a dot of frosting.

Tantalizing Toffee

Makes about 2½ pounds toffee

- 2 cups sugar
- ½ cup water
- ½ cup light corn syrup
- 1 cup butter
- 2¼ cups chopped walnuts, divided
- 1 6-ounce package semisweet chocolate chips

In a 2-quart glass measuring bowl with handle, combine sugar, water, corn syrup, and butter. Microwave at high power (100%) for 5 minutes. Stir to dissolve sugar. Microwave at high power for 16 to 20 minutes or until mixture reaches 300° F. Stir in 1½ cups of the chopped walnuts and quickly spread mixture in a buttered 15- x 10-inch jelly roll pan. Cool. Place chocolate chips in 2-cup glass measure. Microwave at high power for 30 seconds; stir until melted. Spread over cooled toffee. Sprinkle the remaining ¾ cup chopped walnuts over chocolate. Let stand until chocolate is set. Break into pieces.

S'more Bars

Makes 20 bars

- ¾ cup flour
- ¾ cup graham cracker crumbs
- ½ cup sugar
- ½ cup butter, melted
- 1 egg, beaten
- 1 cup miniature marshmallows
- 1 cup coarsely chopped walnuts
- 1 6-ounce package semisweet or milk chocolate pieces

Preheat oven to 350° F. In a large bowl, combine flour, graham cracker crumbs, and sugar. Using a pastry blender, cut in butter until mixture is crumbly. Blend in egg. Spread mixture in a greased 9-inch square pan. Bake for 15 to 20 minutes or until top is lightly browned. Remove from oven; immediately top with marshmallows, walnuts, and chocolate pieces. Return to oven for 2 minutes to soften chocolate. Swirl chocolate over marshmallows and walnuts. Cool until chocolate is set. Cut into bars.

Crisp Chocolate Truffles

Makes 4½ dozen truffles

- 1 7-ounce jar marshmallow creme
- 2 tablespoons butter
- 1 6-ounce package semisweet chocolate chips
- 2 cups puffed rice cereal
- 1 14-ounce package white chocolate coating
- 2 tablespoons vegetable shortening
- Multicolored sprinkles, optional

In a heavy, 2-quart saucepan, combine marshmallow creme, butter, and chocolate chips. Cook over low heat, stirring constantly, until chocolate is melted and mixture is smooth. Remove from heat. Stir cereal into chocolate mixture, mixing until thoroughly combined. Drop by rounded teaspoonfuls onto waxed paper-lined baking sheet. Refrigerate 1 hour or until firm. In top of double boiler, over hot water, melt coating and shortening. Dip each chocolate ball in coating and place on waxed-paper-lined baking sheet. Decorate with sprinkles, if desired. Refrigerate until firm. Place in small candy paper cups to serve.

Photo opposite: Holiday Wreaths, page 18

Breads to Brag About

Upside Down Sticky Muffins

Makes 12 muffins

- ½ cup butter, melted, divided
- ¾ cup firmly packed brown sugar, divided
- 1 teaspoon light corn syrup
- ¾ cup finely chopped walnuts
- 1½ cups flour
- 1 tablespoon baking powder
- 2 teaspoons ground cinnamon
- ¼ teaspoon salt
- 1 egg
- ½ cup milk
- 1 teaspoon vanilla

Preheat oven to 350° F. Lightly grease 12 (2¾-inch) muffin cups. In a small bowl, combine ¼ cup of the butter, ¼ cup of the brown sugar, and corn syrup; mix well. Spoon into muffin cups; sprinkle each with walnuts. In a large bowl, sift together remaining ½ cup brown sugar, flour, baking powder, cinnamon, and salt. Mix well; set aside. In a small bowl, combine remaining ¼ cup butter, egg, milk, and vanilla; blend well. Stir into flour mixture just until dry ingredients are moistened. Spoon over walnuts in muffin cups. Bake 20 minutes or until lightly browned. Remove from oven; loosen edges. Invert onto cooling surface. Place any walnut mixture left in cups on top of muffins.

Pumpkin Bread

Makes 1 loaf

- 2½ cups flour
- 2 teaspoons baking soda
- 1 teaspoon ground cinnamon
- ¼ teaspoon ground nutmeg
- ¼ teaspoon ground cloves
- 1½ cups sugar
- ½ cup vegetable oil
- 1 egg
- 1 16-ounce can pumpkin
- 1 cup chopped walnuts
- ½ cup raisins

Preheat oven to 350° F. Grease a 9- x 5-inch loaf pan. In a small bowl, sift together flour, baking soda, cinnamon, nutmeg, and cloves. Set aside. In a large bowl, combine sugar, oil, and egg; beat until light and fluffy. Stir in pumpkin. Add dry ingredients, a little at a time, beating after each addition. Beat until smooth. Fold in walnuts and raisins. Spoon into pan. Bake 60 to 70 minutes or until toothpick inserted in center comes out clean. Cool in pan 10 minutes. Loosen sides of loaf with a spatula and turn out on wire rack. Wrap tightly with foil or plastic wrap.

Sour Cream Nut Bread

Makes 1 loaf

- 2½ cups buttermilk biscuit mix
- ⅔ cup sugar
- 1 cup chopped nuts
- 1 cup sour cream
- ⅓ cup milk
- 2 eggs, lightly beaten
- 1 teaspoon vanilla

Preheat oven to 350° F. Grease bottom of an 8½- x 4½- x 2½-inch baking pan. In a large bowl, combine biscuit mix, sugar, and nuts. Stir in sour cream, milk, eggs, and vanilla, blending well. Pour into prepared pan. Bake 50 to 55 minutes or until toothpick inserted in center comes out clean. Cool in pan 10 minutes. Remove from pan and cool on wire rack.

Gift Hint

For a special friend, give a cookie jar filled with homemade cookies. Or make your own jar. Spray paint an empty coffee can and stencil on a holiday design or a wish. For a lasting gift, use colors and designs that will harmonize with the recipient's kitchen.

Pineapple Orange Walnut Bread

Makes 1 loaf

- 2 cups flour
- 1 teaspoon baking powder
- ½ teaspoon baking soda
- ¼ teaspoon salt
- ¼ cup butter
- ¾ cup sugar
- 1 egg
- 1 tablespoon grated orange zest
- ¼ cup orange juice
- 1 8-ounce can crushed pineapple
- 1 cup seedless or golden raisins
- 1 cup chopped walnuts, toasted

Preheat oven to 350° F. In a small bowl, sift together flour, baking powder, baking soda, and salt; set aside. In a large bowl, cream butter with sugar until light and fluffy. Beat in egg, orange zest, and orange juice. Alternately stir in flour mixture and undrained pineapple just until blended, ending with flour. Stir in raisins and walnuts. Pour batter into a 9- x 5-inch loaf pan sprayed with vegetable cooking spray. Bake 60 to 70 minutes or until toothpick inserted in center comes out clean. Cool in pan 10 minutes; remove from pan and cool completely on wire rack.

Gift Hint

Cross stitch a saying on the corner of a napkin, line a basket with it, and pile high with homemade muffins. Wrap the whole thing in clear plastic wrap and tie with red ribbon.

Eggnog-Poppy Seed Bread

Makes 1 loaf, 24 slices

- 2½ cups flour
- 1 cup sugar
- 3½ teaspoons baking powder
- 1 teaspoon salt
- 1 teaspoon ground nutmeg
- ¼ cup poppy seed
- 1¼ cups prepared eggnog
- 1 tablespoon plus 1 teaspoon grated orange zest
- 3 tablespoons vegetable oil
- 1 egg

Preheat oven to 350° F. Grease bottom only of a 9- x 5- x 3-inch loaf pan. In a small bowl, sift together flour, sugar, baking powder, salt, and nutmeg. Set aside. In a large bowl, combine all remaining ingredients. Add flour mixture; beat 30 seconds. Pour into pan. Bake 55 to 65 minutes or until toothpick inserted in center comes out clean. Cool slightly. Loosen sides of loaf with a spatula; turn out on a wire rack to cool. Wrap tightly in foil or plastic wrap and refrigerate for up to 1 week.

Cherry Nut Bread with Almond Butter

Makes 1 loaf

- 2 cups flour
- 1 teaspoon baking powder
- ½ teaspoon salt
- ½ cup butter
- 1 cup sugar
- 2 eggs
- 1 10-ounce jar maraschino cherries, drained, reserve juice
- 1 teaspoon vanilla
- ½ cup chopped nuts
- Almond Butter (below)

Preheat oven to 350° F. In a small bowl, sift together flour, baking powder, and salt. Set aside. In a large bowl, cream butter with sugar until light and fluffy. Add eggs, one at a time, beating well after each addition. Measure cherry juice, adding water if necessary, to equal ½ cup. Add flour mixture alternately with cherry juice and vanilla to creamed mixture, mixing well after each addition. Cut cherries in halves and stir into the batter. Stir in nuts. Pour batter into a greased 9- x 5-inch loaf pan. Bake for 60 minutes or until a toothpick inserted in the center comes out clean. Cool in pan 10 minutes. Turn out onto a wire rack to cool completely. Serve with Almond Butter (below).

Almond Butter

- ½ cup butter, softened
- 1 tablespoon finely chopped almonds
- ½ teaspoon almond extract

In a small bowl, blend all ingredients.

Uncommonly Good Cakes

Applesauce Cake

Makes one 10-inch tube cake

- 3 **cups flour**
- 1½ **teaspoon baking soda**
- 1 **teaspoon ground cloves**
- 1 **teaspoon ground nutmeg**
- 1 **teaspoon ground cinnamon**
- ½ **teaspoon salt**
- 1 **cup butter**
- 1 **cup firmly packed brown sugar**
- 1 **cup sugar**
- 2 **eggs**
- 1 **cup applesauce**
- 1 **cup semisweet chocolate chips**
- ½ **cup raisins**
- 1 **cup coconut**
- 1 **cup chopped pecans**

Preheat oven to 350° F. In a small bowl, sift together flour, baking soda, spices, and salt. Set aside. In a large bowl, cream butter with sugars until light and fluffy; add eggs, beating well. Add flour mixture, mixing well. Stir in remaining ingredients and mix well. Pour into greased and floured 10-inch tube pan. Bake 80 to 90 minutes or until toothpick inserted in center comes out clean. Turn out on wire rack to cool. Wrap tightly with foil or plastic wrap to store.

Poppy Seed Cake

Makes one 8-inch round cake

- 2 **cups flour**
- ¼ **teaspoon salt**
- 3½ **teaspoons baking powder**
- ½ **cup shortening**
- 1½ **cups sugar**
- ⅔ **cup poppy seed**
- 1¼ **cups milk**
- 1 **teaspoon almond extract**
- 3 **egg whites**
- **Cream Cheese Icing (below)**

Preheat oven to 360° F. Sift together flour, salt, and baking powder. Set aside. Cream shortening with sugar until light and fluffy. Add poppy seed and mix thoroughly. Add flour mixture alternately with milk, mixing thoroughly after each addition. Stir in almond extract. Beat egg whites until stiff peaks form; fold into batter. Pour into 2 greased and floured 8-inch cake pans. Bake 25 to 30 minutes or until a toothpick inserted in center comes out clean. Cool on wire rack. Frost center and top with Cream Cheese Icing (below).

Cream Cheese Icing

- 1 **3-ounce package cream cheese, softened**
- 1 **tablespoon milk**
- 2½ **cups powdered sugar**
- ½ **tablespoon vanilla**

In a small bowl, combine cream cheese and milk; stir to mix. Add sugar and vanilla, mixing until smooth and creamy.

Jeweled Fruitcake

Makes one 9- x 5-inch loaf

- 1 **cup dried apricots**
- 1 **cup flour**
- ½ **cup sugar**
- ½ **teaspoon baking powder**
- ½ **teaspoon pumpkin pie spice**
- ¼ **teaspoon salt**
- 1½ **cups raisins**
- 1½ **cups Brazil nuts, chopped**
- 1 **cup candied cherries**
- 2 **eggs, beaten**

Preheat oven to 300° F. Cut apricots in half; cover with boiling water and let stand 10 minutes. In a small bowl, sift together flour, sugar, baking powder, pumpkin pie spice, and salt; set aside. Drain apricots. In a large bowl, combine apricots, raisins, nuts, and candied cherries. Add dry ingredients to fruit mixture. Stir in eggs; mix well. Spoon batter into a greased 9- x 5-inch loaf pan; pack down. Garnish with additional candied fruits, if desired. Bake 50 to 60 minutes. Cool on wire rack. When thoroughly cool, wrap tightly with foil or plastic wrap. Let stand overnight before slicing.

Photo opposite: Easy Butter Cake with Tart Lemon Filling, page 27

Cherry Nut Cake

Makes 12 servings

- 2½ cups flour
- 1 tablespoon baking powder
- ¼ teaspoon salt
- 4 egg whites
- ½ cup shortening
- 1½ cups sugar
- ¼ cup juice from maraschino cherries
- 2 teaspoons almond extract
- 1 teaspoon vanilla
- ¾ cup milk
- ½ cup chopped maraschino cherries
- 1½ cup chopped walnuts, divided
- Cherry Frosting (below)

Preheat oven to 350° F. In a small bowl, sift together flour, baking powder, and salt; set aside. In a large bowl, combine egg whites, shortening, and sugar. Beat until light and fluffy. Stir in maraschino cherry juice, almond extract, and vanilla. Add flour mixture alternately with milk, mixing well after each addition. Stir in the cherries and 1 cup of the walnuts. Pour into two greased 9-inch round cake pans. Bake 30 minutes or until toothpick inserted in center comes out clean. Cool in pans 10 minutes. Turn out on wire racks to cool. Frost with Cherry Frosting (below). Sprinkle edge of cake with remaining ½ cup chopped walnuts.

Cherry Frosting

- ¼ cup butter, softened
- 4 cups powdered sugar
- ¼ cup juice from maraschino cherries
- 1 teaspoon vanilla
- ½ teaspoon almond extract

In a small bowl, combine all ingredients; blend until smooth.

Gift Hint

Give a loaf of homemade bread on a breadboard. Wrap it in clear plastic, decorate with ribbon and a sprig of evergreen.

Dump-n-Stir Chocolate Cake

Makes 20 servings

- 2 cups flour
- 2 cups sugar
- 1½ cups unsweetened cocoa
- 2 teaspoons baking powder
- 1 teaspoon baking soda
- ¼ teaspoon salt
- 1½ cups chopped walnuts, optional
- 2 cups milk
- 1 cup vegetable oil
- 2 eggs
- 2 teaspoons vanilla
- Chocolate Frosting (below)
- ¼ cup chopped walnuts, optional

Preheat oven to 350° F. In a large bowl, sift together flour, sugar, cocoa, baking powder, baking soda, and salt. Set aside. In a separate large bowl, combine all remaining ingredients. Add flour mixture and mix well. Pour into greased 13- x 9-inch pan. Bake 40 to 50 minutes or until toothpick inserted in center comes out clean. Cool on wire rack. When cool, frost with Chocolate Frosting (below) and sprinkle with walnuts, if desired.

Chocolate Frosting

- ¼ cup butter, melted
- ½ cup unsweetened cocoa
- 2 tablespoons light corn syrup
- 1 teaspoon vanilla
- 4 cups powdered sugar
- ¼ cup milk

In a small bowl, combine butter, cocoa, corn syrup, and vanilla; blend well. Stir in powdered sugar and milk; mix well.

Packing Hint

When shipping cookies, wrap them singly or in pairs with waxed paper. Pack in layers, cushioning each row of cookies with a generous layer of filler such as popped corn or crumpled newspaper. Use enough filler so the box is very full—the cookies should not have room to bounce around inside. Use a heavy cardboard box that will not be crushed before delivery.

Old Fashioned Brownies

Makes 16 brownies

3 1-ounce squares unsweetened chocolate
½ cup shortening
3 eggs
1½ cups sugar
1½ teaspoons vanilla
¼ teaspoon salt
1 cup flour
1½ cups chopped walnuts, optional

Preheat oven to 325° F. Combine chocolate and shortening in top of double boiler and place over hot (not boiling) water. Stir until melted and blended. Cool slightly. In a large bowl, combine eggs, sugar, vanilla, and salt. Stir in chocolate mixture. Add flour and walnuts. Spread mixture in greased 8-inch square pan. Bake 40 minutes. Brownies should still be soft; do not overbake. Cool completely in pan before cutting.

Fruited Gingerbread

Makes one 9-inch square cake

2 cups flour
2 teaspoons ground allspice
1 teaspoon baking soda
1 teaspoon ground cinnamon
¼ teaspoon salt
½ cup butter, softened
⅔ cup firmly packed brown sugar
2 eggs
½ cup molasses
¾ cup sour cream
1 cup currants
Lemon Sauce (below)

Preheat oven to 325° F. In a small bowl, sift together flour, allspice, baking soda, cinnamon, and salt. Set aside. In a large bowl, cream butter with brown sugar until light and fluffy. Add eggs, one at a time, beating well after each addition. Blend in molasses. Add flour mixture alternately with sour cream, stirring after each addition. Fold in currants. Spoon batter into greased 9-inch square pan. Bake 55 to 60 minutes or until toothpick inserted in center comes out clean. Serve cake warm with Lemon Sauce(below).

Lemon Sauce

½ cup sugar
2 tablespoons cornstarch
1 cup water
3 tablespoons lemon juice
¼ teaspoon grated lemon zest
¼ cup butter

In a small saucepan, combine sugar and cornstarch; mix well. Slowly stir in water, lemon juice, and lemon zest, blending well. Place over medium heat, stirring constantly, until thickened. Remove from heat and stir in butter.

Decadent Holiday Chocolate Torte

Makes 12 servings

3 eggs, separated
⅛ teaspoon cream of tartar
1½ cups sugar
1 cup melted butter
2 teaspoons vanilla
½ cup flour
½ cup cocoa
¼ cup water
1 cup finely chopped pecans
Semisweet Glaze (below)
Holiday candy bits, optional

Preheat oven to 350° F. Line bottom and sides of a 9-inch springform pan with foil. Grease foil. In a small bowl, beat egg whites with cream of tartar until soft peaks form. Set aside. In a large bowl, combine egg yolks, sugar, melted butter, and vanilla. Beat until well blended. Add flour, cocoa, and water. Stir in pecans. Fold reserved egg white mixture into chocolate mixture. Spread into prepared pan. Bake 45 to 55 minutes or until firm to the touch. Cool completely on wire rack. Invert onto serving plate and remove foil. Cover and refrigerate. Spread top and sides with Semisweet Glaze (below). Cover and refrigerate. Press holiday candy bits onto sides, if desired.

Semisweet Glaze

In a small, microwave-safe bowl, combine 1 cup semisweet chocolate chips with ⅓ cup whipping cream. Microwave at high power (100%) for 1 minute. Stir until smooth. Use immediately.

SANTA

Easy Butter Cake with Tart Lemon Filling

Makes 12 to 15 servings

2 cups sifted flour
2 teaspoons baking powder
¾ teaspoon salt
1½ cups sugar
⅔ cups butter, softened
⅔ cup milk
3 eggs
1 teaspoon vanilla
Tart Lemon Filling (below)
Butter Cream Frosting (below)

Preheat oven to 350° F. In a large bowl, sift together flour, baking powder, and salt; stir in remaining ingredients. Beat on low speed for 30 seconds, scraping bowl constantly. On high speed, beat 3 minutes, scraping bowl often. Pour batter into two greased 9-inch round cake pans. Bake 20 to 25 minutes or until cake pulls away from sides of pans and a toothpick inserted in the center comes out clean. Cool on wire racks. Spread Tart Lemon Filling (below) to within ¾ inch of edge of bottom layer. Top with second layer, and frost sides and top with Butter Cream Frosting (below).

Tart Lemon Filling

¾ cup sugar
¼ cup cornstarch
1 cup water
2 egg yolks, slightly beaten
2 tablespoons butter
1 tablespoon grated lemon zest
5 tablespoons lemon juice

In a medium saucepan, combine sugar and cornstarch; gradually stir in water. Place over medium heat, stirring constantly, until mixture thickens and boils. Continue boiling 1 minute. In a small bowl, gradually stir about ½ cup of hot mixture into egg yolks; return egg mixture to saucepan, stirring constantly. Return to boil and cook 1 to 2 minutes, stirring constantly. Remove from heat and continue stirring until smooth. Stir in butter, lemon zest, and lemon juice. Cool.

Butter Cream Frosting

½ cup butter, softened
1 pound powdered sugar, sifted
2 teaspoons vanilla
3 tablespoons milk

In a small bowl, combine all ingredients. Beat with electric mixer on medium speed until well blended.

Mocha Fudge Cake

Makes 12 servings

2 cups flour
½ cup unsweetened cocoa
1 teaspoon baking soda
¼ teaspoon salt
¾ cup shortening
1 cup firmly packed brown sugar
½ cup sugar
2 eggs
1½ cups cold coffee
Mocha Frosting (below)

Preheat oven to 350° F. In a small bowl, sift flour, cocoa, baking soda, and salt. Set aside. In a large bowl, cream shortening with sugars until light and fluffy; beat in eggs. Add flour mixture alternately with coffee, beating after each addition. Pour batter into greased 13- x 9-inch pan. Bake 40 to 45 minutes or until toothpick inserted in center comes out clean. Cool in pan on wire rack. Frost with Mocha Frosting (below).

Mocha Frosting

¼ cup butter
¼ cup unsweetened cocoa
1 teaspoon instant coffee powder
2 tablespoons light corn syrup
2 tablespoons milk
1 teaspoon vanilla
2 cups powdered sugar

In a small saucepan, melt butter. Stir in cocoa and coffee powder until dissolved. Add corn syrup, milk, vanilla, and powdered sugar; beat until smooth and of spreading consistency.

Photo opposite: Santa's Stockings, page 4

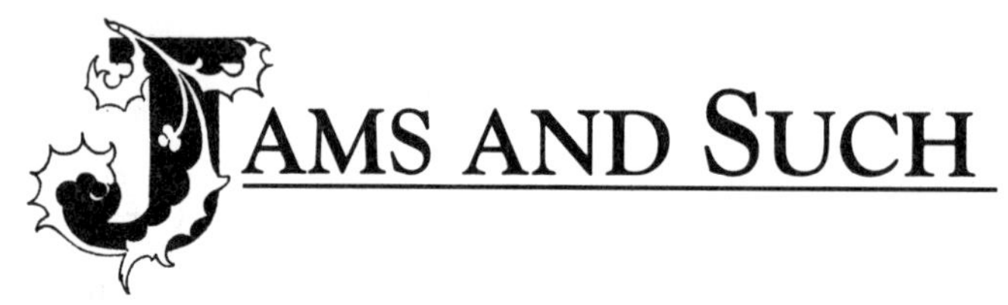

JAMS AND SUCH

NOTE: *Prepare home canning jars and lids according to manufacturer's instructions.*

HAPPY HOLIDAYS CONSERVE

Makes 6 cups

2 30-ounce cans apricot halves
1 cup glacé mixed fruits
½ cup quartered red glacé cherries
1½ cups sugar
¼ teaspoon salt
¼ teaspoon nutmeg
1 tablespoon grated lemon zest
1 tablespoon grated orange zest
1½ cup finely chopped pecans

Drain apricots, reserving 1½ cups syrup. Coarsely chop apricots. In a 6-quart saucepan, combine apricots, apricot syrup, and remaining ingredients except pecans. Bring to a boil, stirring occasionally. Reduce heat; simmer uncovered about 25 minutes or until thickened and of desired consistency. Stir in pecans; ladle into hot, sterilized jars and seal with lid or cover with paraffin according to manufacturer's directions.

SWEET ONION RINGS

Makes 2 to 3 pints

8 cups peeled and sliced onions (about 3 pounds)
1 cup distilled white vinegar
1 cup sugar
2 teaspoons salt
½ teaspoon mustard seed

Place onions in a large saucepan; add enough water to cover. Bring to a boil and boil for 4 minutes; drain. In a separate large saucepan, combine vinegar and remaining ingredients; bring to a boil. Add onions and simmer 4 minutes. Continue simmering while quickly packing clean, hot jars, one at a time. Fill each jar, leaving ½ inch headspace, making certain vinegar solution covers onions. Cap each jar immediately. Process 5 minutes in a boiling water bath.

CHEDDAR CHEESE BALL

Makes 1 ball

1 8-ounce package cream cheese, softened
4 ounces sharp Cheddar cheese, grated
1 tablespoon chopped pimiento
¼ teaspoon cayenne pepper
¼ teaspoon salt
1 tablespoon chopped green pepper
1 teaspoon chopped onion
1½ teaspoon Worcestershire sauce
Red Walnuts (below)

In a small bowl, beat cream cheese until smooth and creamy. Add remaining ingredients except Red Walnuts. Blend well. Shape into a ball and roll in Red Walnuts (below). Wrap tightly in plastic wrap and chill.

RED WALNUTS

½ teaspoon red food color
1½ tablespoons warm water
1 cup finely chopped walnuts

Dissolve food color in water. Sprinkle over walnuts and stir until all nuts are red. Spread nuts on an ungreased cookie sheet and bake at 250° F for 10 to 15 minutes. Do not allow nuts to brown. Turn off oven and leave nuts until completely dry. Cool thoroughly.

BLUE CHEESE

Makes 1 ball

1 8-ounce package cream cheese, softened
4 ounces blue cheese, crumbled
¼ cup chopped green onion
1 teaspoon lemon juice
1 clove garlic, minced
¼ teaspoon pepper
¼ teaspoon salt
½ cup chopped parsley

Combine all ingredients except parsley; blend well. Form mixture into a ball. Roll in chopped parsley. Wrap tightly in plastic wrap and chill thoroughly.

Gingered Pears

Makes about 4 pints

- 3 **4-inch cinnamon sticks**
- 2 **teaspoons whole allspice**
- 1 **teaspoon whole cloves**
- 4 **cups red wine vinegar, 5% acidity**
- 1½ **cups sugar**
  Juice of 1 lemon
- 6 **¼-inch slices fresh gingerroot**
- 5 **pounds ripe pears**

Place cinnamon, allspice, and cloves in a spice bag. In a large saucepan, combine red wine vinegar, sugar, lemon juice, spice bag, and gingerroot. Bring to a boil. Reduce heat and simmer 20 minutes. Peel, halve, and core pears. Heat pears in syrup, one layer at a time. Pack pears into hot jars, with cavity side down and layers overlapping, leaving ½-inch headspace. Carefully ladle hot syrup into jars, leaving ½-inch headspace. Remove air bubbles with a nonmetallic spatula. Wipe jar rim clean. Place lid on jar with sealing compound next to glass. Screw band down evenly and firmly. Do not use excessive force. Process 25 minutes in a boiling-water canner.

Honey Caramel Sauce

Makes 2 cups

- 1 **cup honey**
- 1 **cup evaporated skim milk**
- ½ **cup butter**

In a medium saucepan, combine honey, milk, and butter. Mix well. Cook and stir until mixture comes to a boil. Cook over medium heat 8 to 10 minutes longer or until mixture thickens and turns caramel colored. Pour into sterilized gift jars. Keep refrigerated.

Honey Chocolate Sauce

Makes 2½ cups

- ¾ **cups honey**
- ¾ **cups unsweetened cocoa**
- 2 **tablespoons butter**

Combine all ingredients; mix well. Cover with waxed paper and microwave at high power (100%) 2 to 2½ minutes; stir after 1 minute. Pour into sterilized gift jars. Keep refrigerated.

Honey Turtle Sauce

Makes 3 cups

- 2 **cups Honey Caramel Sauce (above)**
- 1 **cup Honey Chocolate Sauce (above)**
- ¾ **cup broken pecans**

Combine all ingredients and mix well. Pour into sterilized gift jars. Keep refrigerated.

Cranberry Walnut Conserve

Makes about eight 12-ounce jars

- 2 **pounds cranberries, rinsed, drained**
- 3 **cups water**
- 1 **orange, seeded and chopped**
- 2 **large green apples, chopped and cored**
- 1 **cup raisins**
- 1 **package powdered pectin**
- 4 **cups sugar**
- 1 **cup chopped walnuts**
- ½ **teaspoon ground coriander**
- ½ **teaspoon ground allspice**

In a large saucepan, combine cranberries and water. Boil cranberries until they pop. Drain, reserving liquid. Purée cranberries. Combine cranberry purée, reserved liquid, orange, apples, and raisins. Simmer mixture 10 minutes. Stir in pectin; bring to a rolling boil. Add sugar, walnuts, and spices; return mixture to a rolling boil. Boil hard for 1 minute, stirring frequently. Carefully ladle conserve into hot jars, leaving ¼-inch headspace. Wipe jar rim clean. Place lid on jar with sealing compound next to glass. Screw band down evenly and firmly. Do not use excessive force. Process 15 minutes in a boiling-water canner.

Packing Hint

Give jellies in decorative, heat-proof jars or glasses. Label with the variety, date, and your name. Decorate the jar with colorful stickers or photographs of the kind of fruit used in the jelly.

Strawberry Conserve

Makes about five 12-ounce jars

- **2 quarts stemmed, washed strawberries**
- **1 orange, seeded**
- **1 teaspoon lemon juice**
- **1 box powdered pectin**
- **6 cups sugar**
- **1 cup raisins**
- **½ cup sliced almonds**
- **2 teaspoons ground coriander**

Crush strawberries; grind orange. In a large saucepan, combine strawberries, orange, and lemon juice. Place over medium heat; cook and stir for 5 minutes. Stir in powdered pectin. Adjust heat to high and bring to a rolling boil. Boil for 2 minutes, stirring constantly. Add sugar and return to a rolling boil. Boil hard for 1 minute, stirring constantly. Remove from heat and stir in remaining ingredients. Skim foam. Carefully ladle into hot jars. Wipe jar rim clean. Place lid on jar with sealing compound next to glass. Screw band down evenly and firmly. Do not use excessive force. Process 15 minutes in a boiling-water canner.

Maple-Cranberry Syrup

Makes 1½ cups syrup

- **1 cup maple syrup**
- **½ cup whole berry cranberry sauce**
- **¼ cup chopped walnuts, optional**

In a 1-quart saucepan, combine syrup and cranberry sauce. Heat, stirring occasionally, until cranberry sauce is melted. Stir in walnuts, if desired. Serve warm. Store covered in refrigerator up to four weeks.

Packing Hint

Pack an assortment of jellies in a small wooden crate. Attach a wire handle and, if you wish, stencil a holiday greeting on the side slats.

Christmas Berry Jelly

Makes about four 8-ounce jars

- **2 cups apple juice**
- **¼ cup lemon juice**
- **½ cup cinnamon red hots**
- **¾ cup water**
- **1 teaspoon red food color**
- **¼ teaspoon ground mace**
- **1 box powdered pectin**
- **8 whole cloves**
- **1 stick cinnamon**
- **4 cups sugar**

In a large saucepan, combine apple juice, lemon juice, red hots, water, food color, mace, and pectin. Tie cloves and cinnamon stick in a cheesecloth bag. Add bag of spices to juice mixture. Bring to a boil, stirring constantly. Stir in sugar and bring to a full rolling boil. Boil hard for 2 minutes. Remove from heat and skim foam. Carefully ladle hot jelly into hot jars, leaving ¼-inch headspace. Wipe jar rim clean. Place lid on jar with sealing compound next to glass. Screw band down evenly and firmly. Do not use excessive force. Process 5 minutes in a boiling-water canner.

Apple Maple Jam

Makes about seven 8-ounce jars

- **12 cups finely chopped apples**
- **6 cups sugar**
- **1 cup maple syrup**
- **1 teaspoon ground cinnamon**
- **½ teaspoon ground allspice**
- **½ teaspoon ground nutmeg**
- **¼ teaspoon ground cloves**

In a large saucepan, combine all ingredients; slowly bring to a boil. Cook rapidly to 220° F on the thermometer. As mixture thickens, stir frequently to prevent sticking. Carefully ladle into hot jars, leaving ¼-inch headspace. Wipe jar rim clean. Place lid on jar with sealing compound next to glass. Screw band down evenly and firmly. Do not use excessive force. Process 10 minutes in a boiling-water canner.

Photo opposite: Honey Caramel Sauce, page 29

Honey
Caramel Sauce

NDEX

A 1
B 2
C 3
D 4
E 5
F 6
G 7
H 8
I 9
J 0